360⁰ Full Circle Mantra

Your Peace, Your First Priority.

360^0 Full Circle Mantra

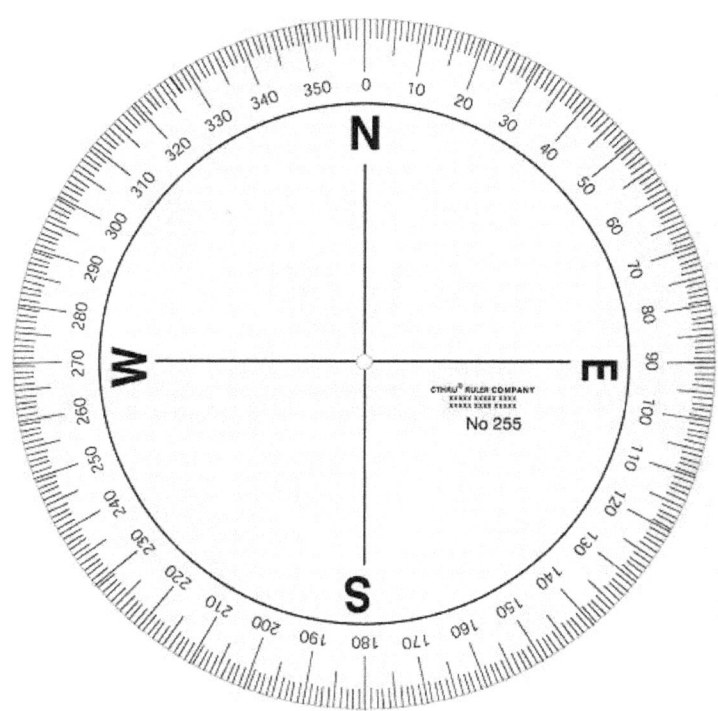

360^0 Full Circle Mantra $A = \pi r^2$

Motseki "Quan" Rabotapi

360^0 Full Circle Mantra

360^0 Full Circle Mantra (Your Peace, Your First Priority)

Copyrights© 2025 by Motseki Rabotapi

Edited by Cathrene Legoete
Cover Design by Motseki "Quan" Rabotapi

Published by Motseki Rabotapi
7681 Mosenogi Str, Extension 1, Khutsong Location,
Carletonville 2499, Merafong City
Gauteng Province, Republic of South Africa
motsekirabotapi@gmail.com
+2776 727 0910

ISBN 978-1-0370-9016-5(print)

All rights reserved. No part of this publication may be reproduced, stored in a retrieval system, or transmitted in any form by any means electronic, mechanical, photocopying, recording or otherwise without the written permission of the copyright owner.

360^0 Full Circle Mantra

$$A = \pi r^2$$

Contents

Acknowledgements 4

Introduction 7

Chapter 1 10

   1^0-90^0 Mantras 10

Chapter 2 29

   91^0-180^0 Mantras 29

Chapter 3 48

   181^0-270^0 Mantras 48

Chapter 4 67

   271^0-360^0 Mantras 67

Conclusion 86

About the Author 88

References 90

Acknowledgements

I'm always grateful for YAH's grace, would not have made it this far without it and I'm nothing without The Most High.

To myself with all the love. Never stop dreaming, named yourself "Navigatah" to take you there…'what you see, you don't like, see what you prefer'.

To my little one, Keabetswe Neo "Mash". Trust your heart nana and live life to the fullest, my love for you can't be expressed through mere words wena neo yaka.

To my mom, Moipone "sisPone". I wish you were here, I miss you more every second I breathe/you resting in peace and forever I accepted you free…

To my dad, Paul "Bra Taps", my lil'bro Mosa "Mitment/Sir Meter" and my lil'sis Kgomotso "Komto/Momo". Thank you so much for the eternal love we share through thick and thin.

To my niece, Naledi "Nels/Nadia Mthethwa". Let your Spirit fly and reach for the stars nana, because that's where your Soul belongs. Love you lots…Mmmbaaa!

To Cathrene"Mamane" "Dipatsi" (LOL). I'm always thankful to have met such a soul that keeps my fire burning any season of our journey. Let's keep making our dreams reality, we got this.

360⁰ Full Circle Mantra

To my nigro, Teboho "Spliff Star". I can't thank you enough bra for keeping me straight, I tip my hat to you! Ngwago re bizzy!

To Xolile "Bhutiza" thank you for being a little brother you are, keep that humble spirit always. Nuff Respekt...Kaa!

To Khanyi "Khanyisile Mbau". Mme your spirit, your heart, your being nje, I can't be thankful enough for your presence in my zone. I will always cherish that Mme.

To Sipho "Cebrelate". I thank you and I appreciate you bra, are phushe mzabalazo. AFRICA is still our motherland! tjovitjooo!

To you the reader. Thank you for giving yourself the time to cultivate yourself. Keep this movement moving, not only for yourself, but also for the next generation. Respekt...YAH Bless!

I'm in control, check, I'm a rolling stone/ my skin tone, can tell I'm a man of my own/ scars in my palms, lessons with open arms/I swear to my moms, can't stop this shooting star/ destined to shine, homeboy, I'm a destiny's child/ Spark in my eye, means home is a sky/ understand I'm a young eagle learning to fly/ and I can tell a difference between a truth and a lie/ love and hate, and what's real and fake/ and I live and sacrifice for project's sake/and before you could let words out of your mouth/ just chill and wait, till I finish building this house/I know y'all cheap talkers, Chicken Little/to see Navigatah later turn to Mr Big Eagle/I never liked short cuts for

360° Full Circle Mantra

References

Motseki "Quan"	Nelson Mandela	Viktor Fronkl
John Eldredge	Puntin	Awokenshit
Sun Tzu	Napoleon Hill	Winnie Nantongo
Winston Churchill	Morgan Olivier	The Project
Bob Marley	Simple Words	Stay Positive
Visualhustles	Scott Clary	Mike Tyson
Charlie Munger	George Shaw	LifeMello
Unknowns	Paulo Coelho	Saraph
Morpheus	Parm k.c	Master Ace
Lao Tzu	Maya Angelou	Bruce Lee
Muhammad Ali	Hopegang	Dark Secrets
Stephen Covey	Blackknowledge	Dolly Parton

360^0 Full Circle Mantra

Use the LINK and QR CODE below.

https://drive.google.com/file/d/1br7S-pCD7mKv1p1fbyrPiwhsNXwbW12u/view?usp=sharing

About the Author

Motseki "Quan"Rabotapi is a father, an author, facilitator & Assessor, Coach and Mentor, Co-Founder of Select Training & Consulting and a Founder of KasiLam'Connekts Booklet. He resides in Khutsong/Carletonville/Merafong City with his siblings Mosa & Kgomotso Rabotapi. He is passionate about nature and personal & community development.

Other Books

own way of change and breathe the fresh air we so desperately require in our lives.

Pause, take a deep breath, reflect and put things in their rightful perspective for your sanity's sake. Meditate on it, pray about it and do whatever it takes to reclaim your peace of mind, spirit and soul. Have words to live by and stand by, let them consume you till you experience the peaceful state that you deserve.

Taste that peace, I guarantee you that you will never ever be the same again. You will be complete.

360^0 Full Circle Mantra read it again, again and again! Till you become it. My gift to you.

M Rabotapi

Conclusion

Anxiety and stress is caused by situations you can't control and try to forcefully control. There isn't a heavy burden in life as trying to change the past and trying to know what the future holds for you. In the meanwhile forgetting that your power is only effective now at this present moment in time.

So most of the time our peace is snatched by not having the right attitude and mind-set to approach the present, to accept and learn from the past and build the future by being aware of the opportunities presented today. A moment ago has already passed, think about it, how then will one harness it back to exploit it? Our attitude is the most important left hook we got, to improve, to deal with, and manipulate our lifestyle.

We spend most of the time whispering words of death and disabling words to our spirit, and that in turn kills the right attitude to have towards living the life we dreaming of.

As you've seen throughout the 360 degrees, we then try to impact our spirit in a positive way and build the relevant attitude of reaching new heights of rearranging our house in order, and set our minds free. And take necessary steps to our fertile present moment and cultivate our future now, peaceful, and getting out of our

Notes:

$356°$

Keep your promise.

Keep your word.

$357°$

You must teach your heart to accept what cannot be changed.

$358°$

Everything in your life is a reflection of a choice you have made, if you want a different result, make a different choice.

$359°$

Prove yourself to yourself.

$360°$

We always work for a better tomorrow, but when tomorrow comes, we again think of a better tomorrow. Let's have a better today as long as it last.

Never get so busy making a living that you forget to make a life and live it.

351^0

Once you learn how to create your own happiness, no one can take it from you.

352^0

One of the healthiest habits to learn: is to take nothing personal.

353^0

Never doubt your purpose, sometimes it just takes time for things to fall into place.

354^0

Appreciate what you have, nobody knows when the last goodbye is.

355^0

Anyone can say they care, but watch their actions not their words.

345^0

Either you find a way or you make a way. Stop complaining.

346^0

Always be careful when you follow the masses, sometimes the "m" is silent.

347^0

Give yourself time.

348^0

Be strong enough to stand alone, smart enough to know when you need help, and brave enough to ask for it.

349^0

The world is changed by your example not by your opinion.

350^0

360° Full Circle Mantra

Fuck people! Everyone has an opinion about everything. You will go crazy trying to please everyone, don't even try. Listen, smile, agree and then do whatever the fuck you were going to do anyway.

341°

May you heal from things you don't talk about.

342°

It's not healthy to hear complaints, judgement and negative things all the time. Be careful with the information you receive and take care of your Spirit.

343°

Mistakes are proof that you are trying.

344°

You have good days and you have bad days, that's life.

$335°$

Don't be ashamed of your hustle, people will not put food on your table or pay your bills.

$336°$

Remember, YAH never closes one door without opening another door. Stop staring at the closed door.

$337°$

Sometimes the right path is not the easiest one.

$338°$

Reset. Restart. Refocus as many times as you need to.

$339°$

We only have one life to live and short time to live it.

$340°$

The place that inspires you.

330^0

Don't judge a situation you have never been in.

331^0

Being deeply loved by someone gives you strength, while loving someone deeply gives you courage.

332^0

Learn to be done, not mad, not bothered, just done. Protect your peace at all cost.

333^0

Travel and tell no one, live a true love story and tell no one, live happily and tell no one. People can ruin beautiful things.

334^0

If you don't heal from what hurt you, you will bleed on people who didn't cut you.

$325°$

Forgiving people in silence and never talking to them again is a form of self-care. Remember that.

$326°$

When a flower doesn't bloom, you fix the environment in which it grows, not the flower.

$327°$

First treat them how you want to be treated, then treat them how they treat you.

$328°$

Look around you, there is always something to be grateful for.

$329°$

There are two places you need to go often:

The place that heals you.

$319°$

You don't decide your future, you decide your habits that decides your future.

$320°$

Above all, don't lie to yourself.

$321°$

You are not behind in life, your journey is just different.

$322°$

People won't understand your perspective, and that is completely fine.

$323°$

Help someone without telling everyone about it.

$324°$

Sitting in your own space in peace, eating snacks and minding your own business is priceless.

$360°$ Full Circle Mantra

Never argue with someone who believes their own lies.

$314°$

Sometimes you have to do it yourself if you want it done.

$315°$

Don't compare yourself with others, everyone has their own role to play.

$316°$

Be teachable and be open, you're not always right.

$317°$

Sugar and salt look the same, be careful who you trust.

$318°$

You become who you surround yourself with.

$308°$

Everyone you meet is fighting a battle you know nothing about. Be kind always.

$309°$

If you don't sacrifice for what you want, what you want becomes the sacrifice.

$310°$

Notice the people who loves you when loving yourself is difficult. They deserve a special place in your life.

$311°$

Not everyone will see your vision.

$312°$

If you ask a question, you are a fool for a minute. If you don't ask, you will be a fool for life.

$313°$

Let people do what they want to do, so you'd see what they would rather do. That will answer all the questions you have.

304^0

You let bad days affect you too much. You don't let your good days affect you enough. Fix that.

305^0

If you're not careful in this life, rumours will make you hate the innocent ones and love the hypocrites.

306^0

You don't have to react to everything. Just sit back and watch clowns do what clowns do best.

307^0

Don't wait to make your dreams come true, because one day it might be too late.

$298°$

Don't use your energy to worry. Use it to believe in your capabilities.

$299°$

Helping one person might not change the whole world, but it could change the world for that one person.

$300°$

If you close your eyes to facts, you will learn through accidents.

$301°$

There is a difference between knowing the path and walking the path.

$302°$

You don't truly know someone until you fight them.

$303°$

You are the one that's got to die when is time for you to die, so live your life the way you want to.

293^0

Pay attention to the way you feel around people. Energy never lies.

294^0

Don't let the internet rush you, no one is posting their failures and setbacks.

295^0

What's meant for you will always feel natural, calm and clear, not forced, chaotic and confused.

296^0

Don't take revenge. The rotten fruit will fall by themselves.

297^0

Don't hurt yourself trying to fit in.

287^0

You glow different when you have good people with good intentions in your life.

288^0

Appreciate where you are in your journey, even if it's not where you want to be. Every season serves a purpose.

289^0

Recognise, if they want to, they will.

290^0

You can get fired from a job, but you can't get fired from your gift. Find your gift and you'll always have work.

291^0

Remember, a diamond is a coal that did well under pressure.

292^0

Your eye will never forget what your heart has seen.

282^0

Birds born in a cage, think flying is an illness.

283^0

Home is not where you live. Home is where you belong.

284^0

Let whoever think whatever, just keep getting better.

285^0

Sometimes in life you just need a hug. No words, no advice, just a hug.

286^0

Give your brain as much attention as you do to your hair, face, nails and body.

The wrong friend will hold you back, but the right friend pushes you to be better.

276^0

One of the best lessons you can learn in life is to master the art of how to remain calm.

277^0

Allow someone to love you.

278^0

Be proud of your progress and keep taking steps forward no matter how small.

279^0

Stop wasting time.

280^0

"I'll do it tomorrow" is a disease that will kill your dreams.

281^0

Chapter 4
271^0-360^0 Mantras

271^0

The best thing about the worst time of your life is that you get to see the true colours of everyone.

272^0

Some things no longer belong in your life. Let them go and trust that what comes next will be better than what's just left.

273^0

If you are right, no one remembers. If you are wrong, no one forgets. Accept it.

274^0

Sometimes you just have to walk alone, to see who's willing to walk with you.

275^0

Notes:

That move you scared to take, just might be the one that will change your destiny.

266^0

You don't stop having fun because you get old, you get old because you stop having fun.

267^0

If you can do something about it, do it! Instead of thinking about it.

268^0

You don't know how fast time goes by, till you get there.

269^0

Sometimes what didn't work out for you, really worked out for you.

270^0

Think of each day as a single life.

$260°$

Healing yourself can be offensive to people that benefit from your brokenness.

$261°$

Never stop learning, because life never stops teaching.

$262°$

Work hard in silence let your success be your noise.

$263°$

Sometimes you need your feelings hurt, so you can wake up and focus on you and your goals.

$264°$

Be with someone who says…"Let's fix it, I can't lose you"

$265°$

Focus on the support that keeps showing up, not who you thought would show up.

255^0

People don't care for you when you are alone, they just care for you when they are alone.

256^0

There is always a way to reach out and love.

257^0

Choose the one who chooses you above all others, and can tell you all the reasons why.

258^0

We make time for the things we love, and excuses for the things we don't. Simple and plain!

259^0

How others sees you is not important, how you see yourself means everything.

$249°$

The fears we don't face becomes our limits.

$250°$

Before you build for others, build your castle first.

$251°$

The people who truly cares for you, won't have to tell you they care, they will show you.

$252°$

Watch how peaceful life gets when you raise the bar on who has access to you.

$253°$

No response is a response, and it is a powerful one. Remember that.

$254°$

Don't waste another year by doing the same mistakes.

244^0

Old ways don't open new doors.

245^0

Death is not the greatest loss in life. The greatest loss in life is what dies inside us while we still alive.

246^0

Sometimes the place you are used to is not the place you belong to.

247^0

Never let the same snake bite you twice.

248^0

The key is to keep company only with people who uplift you, whose presence calls forth your best.

Every problem is a gift, without problems we would not grow.

238^0

You can shape yourself exactly how you like.

239^0

Optimism is the best way to see life.

240^0

You don't learn from winning. You learn from losing.

241^0

Love what you have before life teaches you to love what you lost.

242^0

Money makes a difference, learn to make some.

243^0

$232°$

They start missing you when they fail to replace you.

$233°$

Believe what your heart tells you, not what others say.

$234°$

Take risk: if you win, you will be happy and if you lose, you will be wise.

$235°$

Devote the rest of your life to making progress.

$236°$

Tomorrow will never come, do it now...today.

$237°$

Never get too attached to someone unless they feel the same about you. Because one sided expectations can mentally destroy you.

228^0

Your freedom will begin when you come to a point where you have no need to impress anyone, but yourself.

229^0

A mistake is your teacher, not your enemy. A mistake is a lesson, not a loss. It's a temporary detour, not a dead-end.

230^0

When you choose peace it comes with a lot of goodbyes.

231^0

Some talk to you in their free time and some free their time to talk to you. Know the difference.

The gap between the life you want and the life you're living is called mind-set, focus and consistency.

223^0

Once you realise you deserve the best, losing people from your life won't affect you anymore.

224^0

Cry as much as you want to, but make sure when you stop crying, you'll never cry again for the same reason.

225^0

You get what you focus on, so focus on what you want.

226^0

Be patient when becoming someone you haven't been before.

227^0

Stay away from "still" people, still complaining, still hating, still not grown, still nowhere.

218^0

Give people time, give people space, don't beg anyone to stay, let them roam. What's meant for you will always be yours.

219^0

The most powerful motivation is rejection.

220^0

Die with memories not with dreams.

221^0

Never underestimate your light. It may be your light that leads others out of the darkness.

222^0

$213°$

If your absence doesn't bother them, then your presence never mattered to them in the first place.

$214°$

Angry people want you to see how powerful they are. Loving people want you to see how powerful you are.

$215°$

You can do 99 things for someone and all they'll remember is the 1 thing you didn't do for them.

$216°$

Self-doubt kills more dreams than failure ever will.

$217°$

Sometimes you have to do what is best for you and your life, not what's best for everyone else.

209^0

Don't be upset when people reject you. Nice things are rejected all the time by people who can't afford them.

210^0

Forget your age, if you have dreams to achieve, you still young.

211^0

3 hobbies you must have:

- One to keep you creative.
- One to keep you in shape.
- One to make you money.

212^0

Victory comes from finding opportunities in problems.

$360°$ Full Circle Mantra

$204°$

Hungry stomach, empty pocket and a broken heart can teach you the best lessons of life.

$205°$

Never be a prisoner of your past, it was just a lesson not a life sentence.

$206°$

Sometimes the smallest step in the right direction ends up being the biggest step of your life.

$207°$

If you tell the truth, it becomes a part of your past. But if you lie, it becomes a part of your future.

$208°$

$198°$

Learn to fight alone.

$199°$

The climb is tough, but the view from the top is worth it.

$200°$

Today is your day.

$201°$

Face your fears, eat wealthy, exercise, admit your mistakes, refine your goals and believe it's possible.

$202°$

Don't lose hope, you never know what tomorrow will bring.

$203°$

Kill your excuses and face your fears head on.

$192°$

Once you carry your own water, you will learn the value of every drop.

$193°$

Happiness depends on your attitude, not on what you have.

$194°$

Normalise "I am willing to work on that" instead of "that's just how I am".

$195°$

Work until you no longer have to introduce yourself.

$196°$

Be who you want to be, not what others want to see.

$197°$

Take the risk, or lose the chance.

Listen to people when they are angry, that's when the real truth comes out.

187^0

Never plan a future with people who don't have future plans.

188^0

You can be the only reason why someone still keeps holding on.

189^0

When there is a will, there is a way.

190^0

Sunset is more colourful than sunrise. Sometimes good things happen in goodbyes.

191^0

Never underestimate the importance of small steps.

Chapter 3
181^0-270^0 Mantras

181^0

First they laugh, then they watch, then they copy. Be aware.

182^0

You don't always attract what you are. You sometimes attract people who are in desperate need of what you are.

183^0

Let kids choose their own future.

184^0

Don't lose your mind over people who don't mind losing you.

185^0

You learn nothing from life if you think you are right all the time.

186^0

Notes:

We are born in 1 day. We die in 1 day. We can change in 1 day. We can fall in love in 1 day. Anything can happen in just 1 day. You only have just 1 day.

177^0

Stop getting distracted by things that have nothing to do with your goals.

178^0

Be careful what you tolerate, you are teaching people how to treat you.

179^0

Realise silence is more powerful than proving a point.

180^0

Only those who care about you can hear you when you are silent.

Never judge the future of a person based on their present condition, because time has the power to turn any black coal to a shiny diamond.

172^0

Don't force things. What flows, flows. What crashes, crashes. Have space and energy for things that are meant for you.

173^0

Know that the day you plant the seed isn't the day you eat the fruit.

174^0

Sadly, the only way some people will learn to appreciate you is by losing you.

175^0

Be kind to the past version of yourself that didn't know the things you now know.

176^0

If you don't like the road you are walking on at this moment, start paving another one.

168^0

You become your best self when you work on things that people can't take away from you.

169^0

3 things to keep private…

- Your love life.
- Your income.
- Your next move.

170^0

Getting married after 30 is still beautiful. Starting a family after 35 is still possible. Buying a house after 40 is still a boss move. Don't let people rush you with their timeline.

171^0

162^0

Stop thinking and start doing.

163^0

Don't force anyone to be like you.

164^0

If you want to be good at something, you need to remain a student always.

165^0

No matter what your current circumstances are, if you imagine something better for yourself, you can create it.

166^0

Don't let other peoples' opinions shape what you think is acceptable and what's not.

167^0

$156°$

Don't allow someone else to kill your dream. If you can see it in your mind, you can do it.

$157°$

Life begins where fear ends.

$158°$

If you cannot do great things, do small things in a great way.

$159°$

Just let time unfold the truth.

$160°$

Learn to delete anything in your mind that isn't moving you forward.

$161°$

Some problems can be solved by working together.

$150°$

If you let a person talk long enough you'll hear their true intentions.

$151°$

Not every place you fit in, is where you belong.

$152°$

It's ok not to be in the spotlight.

$153°$

Freedom comes with sacrifice.

$154°$

Never reply when you are angry.

Never make a promise when you are happy.

Never make a decision when you are sad.

$155°$

If your net is not in the water, you won't be catching any fish.

Know the difference between those who stay to feed the soil and those who come to grab the fruit.

145^0

Decide what you want, write it down, make a plan and work on it every single day.

146^0

Change is very hard but it's necessary.

147^0

Don't be afraid of being different, be afraid of being the same as everyone else.

148^0

If there is a book you really want to read but it hasn't been written yet, then you must write it yourself.

149^0

Don't let your loyalty become slavery.

Challenges are what makes life interesting, overcoming them is what makes life meaningful. Don't stop challenging yourself.

141^0

Excuses make today easy, but tomorrow hard.

Discipline make today hard, but tomorrow easy.

Ask yourself if what you doing today is getting you closer to where you want to be tomorrow.

142^0

The problem is…you think you have time.

143^0

Learn to be present and enjoy the moment.

144^0

$135°$

Happiness is not about getting all you want but it's about enjoying all you have.

$136°$

Sometimes the things that are holding you back are all in your mind.

$137°$

Every problem has its solution. But if you don't talk, no one can help you.

$138°$

Nobody is busier than a person not interested in you.

$139°$

Money doesn't change people, it just amplifies who you really are.

$140°$

Show appreciation to the people who loves you unconditionally.

130^0

Don't judge others, you don't know what kind of situations they are facing in their life.

131^0

Your words starts to lose value when your actions don't match.

132^0

The best project you'll ever work on is **YOU**.

133^0

Never get too attached to something that isn't yours.

134^0

Don't tell anyone to get over it, assist them to get through it instead.

124^0

If they come back to your life, don't forget how they left.

125^0

Nobody cares. Worry about yourself, your family and people that are important to you.

126^0

The past is your lesson.

The present is your gift.

The future is your motivation.

127^0

Pain changes people.

128^0

Get up or give up...you decide.

129^0

Sometimes the person who do the work doesn't appear in the picture.

118^0

Sometimes you have to move on without certain people, if they're meant to be in your life, they'll catch up.

119^0

Don't stop dreaming just because you had a nightmare.

120^0

Be your best and forget the rest.

121^0

Efforts are better than promises.

122^0

Never burn yourself to keep others warm.

123^0

All things are hard before they get easy.

You have to experience life to understand it.

112^0

If the plan doesn't work, change the plan not the goal.

113^0

When you think about giving up, just think how far you've come.

114^0

Sometimes you have to risk it all for a vision no one else can see but you.

115^0

I hope you know you are doing better than you think you are.

116^0

A short walk can make a huge difference.

117^0

$106°$

Don't go broke helping everyone because when you go broke nobody is going to help you.

$107°$

As long as you know your heart and intentions are pure, don't try to explain yourself to anyone.

$108°$

You don't have to announce it, you can just change your life.

$109°$

If it cost you your peace then the price is too high.

$110°$

If you haven't tasted a bad apple, you won't appreciate a good one.

$111°$

insecurities. Start with what you know already. Start small....JUST START!

101^0

Learn and apply.

102^0

Wrong is wrong, even if everyone is doing it.

Right is right, even if no one is doing it.

103^0

Don't let peer pressure dictate your next move.

104^0

A dream will be a dream until action makes it a reality.

105^0

Every next level of your life will demand a different version of you.

360° Full Circle Mantra

You learn quickly when you do a mistake, so perfectionism won't do you any good. Just take a look at children.

96°

You have the power to make anything happen, but you must act now.

97°

One day it will all make sense. Be patient.

98°

Always ask yourself why first, what's in it for you?

99°

If you want to know someone's mind, listen to their words. And if you want to know their heart, watch their actions.

100°

Start now! Start where you are. Start with what you have. Start with all your

Chapter 2
91^0-180^0 Mantras

91^0

Remove some foods, remove some people and remove some habits in your life, and see how some problems vanishes right before your eyes.

92^0

Be a good person, but don't waste your time proving it.

93^0

Do what you have to do until you do what you want to do.

94^0

Accept people as they are, but place them where they belong. Hire, fire and promote accordingly as you are the CEO of your life.

95^0

360^0 Full Circle Mantra

Notes:

$88°$

Always choose yourself first and then choose who chooses you.

$89°$

Never blame anyone in your life, good people will bring happiness and bad people will bring experience.

$90°$

At some point you just have to let go of what you thought should happen and live in what is happening now.

If it comes to you, welcome it with both hands. And if it goes away from you, let it.

83^0

All endings are also new beginnings.

84^0

Never ever forget who helped you in difficult times, who put you in difficult times and most importantly who left you in difficult times.

85^0

Change your mind set and you'll change your life.

86^0

The whole staircase is a lot more easier when you focus on the step in front of you.

87^0

Ideas without actions are nothing.

it. If you don't want to eat it, just don't eat it. If you don't want to buy it, don't buy it.

78^0

Don't expect anything from anyone, if you are being considered be grateful for it.

79^0

It's never too late...to start again. To build, to rebuild, to finish what you've started, as long as you still breathing.

80^0

Everyone has their own timeline, don't compare yours with others. Age don't mean shit!

81^0

No one knows everything, but try to take heed of good advice from both the young and old.

82^0

You can only control your thoughts, feelings and actions. No one is a puppet.

75^0

A closed door if opened, it's a good thing but if it kept closed regardless of your efforts, leave it alone and focus on another door.

76^0

Only look back for the purpose of learning a lesson and embarrassing that moment but not trying to relive the experience because you'll be blind to appreciate the present moment.

77^0

Don't force yourself to do anything you don't want to do. If you don't want to go, don't go. If you don't want to do it, don't do it. If you don't want to wear it, don't wear

LOVE! You can only see the beauty of it if you allow yourself to love.

70^0

If you want to be in control of your life, create your own storyline.

71^0

If you think you don't have time, MAKE TIME!

72^0

When you have an anxiety, the only thing that's real is what's in the present moment in time, what is happening now. Focus on the present moment.

73^0

Stop pretending as if you ok, accept it and you'll be free. Hope for the best.

74^0

360^0 Full Circle Mantra

64^0

It's ok not to be ok, cry if you have to, and just let it out.

65^0

Ask, seek and knock...continuously, till you get an answer, you find and the door is opened for you.

66^0

Don't just watch with your eyes but SEE, don't just listen with your ears but HEAR!

67^0

We all have the power of will to choose.

68^0

Your brain is there for you to think with and comprehend, and your heart is there for you to live from.

69^0

Sometimes you just need a little dash of patience in your life.

59^0

Find your own identity and you'll find yourself.

60^0

Just know you are the way you are because someone needs you and wishes to be blessed by someone like you in their life.

61^0

What if you're right and it works? What if?

62^0

Don't let that kid in you suffocate. Let it gasp for air and breath.

63^0

Forgive yourself, you did not know any better yesterday.

52^0

If you can do it, do it. And if you can't do it, learn how to do it.

53^0

Take that leap of faith, take that first step, and make that first move.

54^0

Find something to believe in and fight and die for it.

55^0

Growth comes when you become a student.

56^0

Find someone who believes in you, you only need one! And look at your life flourish.

57^0

Do what makes you come alive.

58^0

Just jump into the unknown, you'll figure things out on the way.

47^0

JUST DO IT!!!

48^0

Let people be, you can't control anybody's actions or reactions. Whether you like it or not, people will do whatever they want.

49^0

Dare yourself and do what's scares you. You going to learn a lot about yourself.

50^0

"I'll think about it." Is very important, say it more often.

51^0

Any favour you accept to do for anyone, it'll be a full responsibility forfeited to you.

41^0

Don't waste your time trying to explain yourself, people understand what they want to understand.

42^0

Know defeat and know victory.

43^0

Don't box yourself in, but stay true to your word.

44^0

Say what you mean and mean what you say.

45^0

Don't inherit anyone's fear, as no one has done it before and yet everyone says it can't be done. As long as you see it, it can be done.

46^0

Overthinking can steal the true sense of reality.

36^0

Don't be afraid to build, to tear down and rebuild.

37^0

Life is fused with tests and lessons, let them build your character.

38^0

Don't be hush to yourself, you are only human.

39^0

If there's anything that makes your spirit burn with excitement...DO IT!

40^0

Explore Life. That is true adventure! Crawl, walk, run, jump, climb and lay down.

360^0 Full Circle Mantra

29^0

Run your own race. Run on your own lane. Run with your own pace.

30^0

When you love...LOVE!

31^0

Let go of what was, embrace what is and have faith for what will be.

32^0

The cave you afraid of, has everything you wished for.

33^0

Keep what's supposed to be kept and throw away what's supposed to be thrown away.

34^0

Be honest to yourself.

35^0

Mind your own business. Mind your own life. Mind your own time. As you have so much to do to improve on the quality of your own life.

24^0

Energy or Vibration never lie. Sense or feel it. You'll know what time is it.

25^0

Some good-byes are good for your soul.

26^0

If not now, when? If not you, then who?

27^0

Your down-time space is a true reflection of yourself. Take a look at your space, That Is You.

28^0

There's only one life to live and short time to live it. Make it count.

If you truly love someone, tell them. If you don't like them, keep your goddamn mouth shut!

19^0

If you can assist, don't wait for another minute, just offer to help.

20^0

Smile, Laugh, Cry, Empathies and be Angry, all these emotions shows you are a human being.

21^0

Don't waste your energy trying to build a pond in the middle of the desert.

22^0

Try, just try and you'll realise there was nothing to worry about.

23^0

13^0

If you are broke, you are not poor.

14^0

Only the Most High is perfect, forgive yourself and others. But there are those who deserve punishment once in a while.

15^0

Learn from your mistakes. As they are only that...MISTAKES!

16^0

If you were the wrong one, apologise. If they were the wrong ones, understand we are all human beings. If it continues, know it's deliberate and cut yourself off.

17^0

Don't wait for the perfect time, as the only time is guaranteed is NOW!

18^0

$7°$

Listen to understand.

$8°$

Be an empty cup, you'll learn a lot and be wise.

$9°$

Gratitude. Be thankful for every little thing you have, as someone wishes to be as blessed as you are.

$10°$

If you are not invited, don't go. If you are invited, don't over stay your welcome.

$11°$

If you are not informed, don't ask.

$12°$

Don't pretend as if you know or understand, just ask for clarity to the person who was sharing the information.

Chapter 1
$1°$-$90°$ Mantras

$1°$

Know YOURSELF. Know exactly who YOU are.

$2°$

Know YOUR enemy.

$3°$

Know YOUR place in people's lives.

$4°$

Stop trying to control everything and let go.

$5°$

Eat and Plan to eat with people who eats and plans to eat with you.

$6°$

Learn to say …NO!

360^0 Full Circle Mantra

You then need to create and set aside some time for yourself. And have a special meeting with yourself, every single day of your life. To encourage, to discipline, to motivate, to assess, to give "high-five", to report, to challenge yourself always.

This is a collective of building blocks of quotes that helped me in so many ways to stretch my mind, and wanted to share with you that they might also assist and impact in some way or the other in your life as well. There is nothing that can beat having the right tools for the job, also as having the right mind-set to tackle and face life. For life, you need the right angles to live it to the fullest and enjoy its lessons and changes, twists and turns.

Let journey together through this maze of life with these 360 mantra and try to complete our circle of peace.

Introduction

Do you often talk to yourself? Wait a minute! How often do you talk to yourself? How important it is to you to talk to yourself? And what is it that you constantly talking to yourself about?

If you can't have a conversation with yourself about yourself, who then is responsible for you? Who's supposed to fit in those shoes? The unfortunate part of it, is that, those kinds of shoes are not "the one-size-fits-all" kind of shoes, they were meant for you. They were designed for you, and on top of that, they were moulded to fit only one person and one person only. And that person is **You**!

By that being said, why is it important to have conversations with yourself? Why is it such a big fuss about it? If you think about it, we are simply created to solve problems or become solutions. We then are required to constantly fixing, creating, destroying and rebuilding any situation we come across. Easier said than done right…yep! So we need to stretch our thinking capacity, as our mind is designed to be elastic, and can adopt to any situation. Our mind is basically a muscle that needs exercising to develop. Thinking and pondering, reading and new and old experiences are those exercises we need to build and flex this muscle of ours.

360⁰ Full Circle Mantra

traveling reasons/ I took a road not taken for personal reasons….
What you want? **The Project**